What is Kosher?

An Introduction to the Laws of Kashrut

Rabbi Juan Bejarano Gutierrez

DEDICATION

To my beautiful wife who always supports me and encourages me in my writing and research.

CONTENTS

ACKNOWLEDGMENTS

I would like to thank four rabbis who have impacted me over the years. Rabbi Byron Sherwin z"l at the Spertus Institute for Jewish Learning and Leadership influenced my understanding of Judaism profoundly. His class lectures were not only academic but the starting point of deep reflection. I was particularly saddened by his passing. His influence will remain with me.

Rabbi Victor Beck, z"l was extremely gracious and encouraging at my wedding and always helped me in my rabbinical studies. Rabbi David Roller taught me the realities of synagogue life that have proven correct over the years. I would also like to thank Rabbi Frank Joseph of the Irving Havurah, who embraces everyone with a positive attitude and is an example of kindness and compassion to all who know him.

My heartfelt thanks and love go to my wife who supports my research and writing.

CHAPTER 1
WHY KASHRUT?

Traditional Judaism holds that the Torah was revealed by Moses to the Jewish people in both written and oral forms at Mount Sinai. The written form is referred to as the *Torah She'biktav,* literally the Torah which is written. The written Torah consists of the Five Books of Moses which are the first five books of the Bible (i.e. Genesis, Exodus, Leviticus, Numbers, and Deuteronomy). The oral form is referred to as the *Torah She'be'al Peh*, literally the Torah of the mouth and is found in a legal code known as the Mishnah and it's associated commentary which comprises the Talmud. The Torah, in its written and oral form, serves as the guidepost by which a traditional Jewish life is understood and practiced.

The term *Kashrut* refers to the Jewish religious dietary laws derived from the Torah. The term *kashrut* is derived from the Hebrew word *kasher* meaning fit or acceptable. From the word *kasher*, we derive the word *kosher* in its anglicized form. But before we discuss what kosher is, let's discuss some ideas as to "why" kosher exists. Why after all, would a religious faith be concerned about what people eat? Answering this may seem complicated at first, but I believe it's important to understand the "whys" before the "hows".

The Rationale for Kashrut

What is interesting if not mind-boggling to many is that the Torah does not specifically state why the dietary laws were given. Because the Torah does not mention the reasons for the dietary laws, many individuals spend a lot of time trying to determine a rationale for their existence, and their relevance in a modern society. After all, if something is so important, why isn't the ultimate purpose clear?

The Torah does not oblige in such efforts, however. While the Torah tells the history of the Jewish people, it also contains various laws that describe and detail the terms of the covenant between G-d and the People of Israel. Understanding the different types of commandments can be helpful in appreciating the actions and prohibitions the Torah mentions. This, in turn, may help us understand the reason the dietary laws exist. The written Torah includes three types of commandments. These are typically divided into *mishpatim* (laws or judgments), *chukkim* (decrees), and *eidot* (testimonials or signs).[1]

Mishpatim

The word *Mishpatim* is the plural form of the word *Mishpat* which means judgment. *Mishpatim* are often regarded as those commandments whose value is understood through simple reason. For example, the value of prohibiting adultery, theft, or

---

[1] "The Two Faces of A Mitzvah." - Passover. Accessed March 03, 2016. http://www.chabad.org/holidays/passover/pesach_cdo/aid/1718/je wish/The-Two-Faces-of-A-Mitzvah.htm.

murder to any civilized society is generally obvious and the benefit of these prohibitions is universally recognized regardless of a person's religious or cultural tradition. In short these commandments are, for lack of a better term, *logical* commandments.[2]

Eidot

Eidot, are commandments that serve to commemorate an event or represent something. The commandments to put on *tefillin*[3] or eat *matzah* (unleavened bread) on Passover are perfect examples of *Eidot*.[4] The case of the Passover meal is perhaps the most pronounced of these. Because of its significance, I will elaborate briefly on the story of Passover.

The meaning of Passover is connected to the Exodus from Egypt which is fundamental to the Jewish faith. The Ten

---

[2] See Maimonides' *Moreh Nevuchim* Chapter 26.

[3] i.e. small black leather boxes containing scrolls of parchment. The scrolls are inscribed with verses from the Torah. They are worn by religious Jews during weekday morning prayers.

[4] "The Logic of the Mitzvot." Parshah RSS. Accessed March 03, 2016. http://www.chabad.org/parshah/article_cdo/aid/2797/jewish/The-Logic-of-the-Mitzvot.htm.

Commandments begin with: "I am the L-rd your G-d who (*because I*) brought you out of the land of Egypt."[5] The Jewish people believe in the Torah because of its collective memory of the Exodus from Egypt.[6] The *Passover Seder* is a meal in which the story of the Jewish people and their journey to, settlement, enslavement, and finally redemption from Egypt is retold on a yearly basis. I believe it is worth noting, that the Passover story reflects one of the great innovations of Biblical religion. The Bible placed the emphasis on historical narratives in contrast to other ancient near eastern religions which emphasized nature. As the Jewish theologian, Abraham Joshua Heschel noted, for Judaism *faith is memory*. On the importance of memory, he stated:

> "When we want to understand ourselves, to find
>
> out what is most precious in our lives, we search

---

[5] Exodus 20:2.

[6] Most importantly Rabbi Byron Sherwin stated: "But memory does not merely signify mental recall, but includes a call to action. Not affirmation of dogmas but evocation of deeds is the meaning of this term. Liturgy and ritual serves as vehicles to prevent memory from deteriorating into an abstract reminiscence...As Abraham Joshua Heschel put it, 'An esthetic experience leaves behind the memory of a perception and enjoyment; a prophetic experience leaves behind the memory of commitment.'" Byron L. Sherwin, *Faith Finding Meaning* (New York: Oxford, 2009), 100-101.

our memory…That only is valuable in our experience which is worth remembering. Remembrance is the touchstone of all actions. Memory is a source of faith. To have faith is to remember. Jewish faith is a recollection of that which happened to Israel in the past…Recollection is a holy act; we sanctify the present by remembering the past."[7]

The observance of the Passover Seder is, therefore, an affirmation of Jewish faith through memory. The ritual attached to that sacred event is an enactment of faith. All Jewish holidays reflect an event or episode in Israel's history which is connected to a certain theological belief.[8] The sacred texts of Israel establish the religious imperative of remembering for the entire Jewish community. The Biblical concern with memory is tied to the notion of a holy history, and hence a holy people.

Kiddush, the ritual blessing over a cup of wine or grape juice on

---

[7] Abraham Joshua Heschel, *Man is Not Alone* (Philadelphia: Jewish Publication Society, 1951), 162-163.

[8] Another example is *Rosh Hashanah*, the Jewish New Year, which commemorates the creation of the world, the binding of Isaac, etc.

Shabbat (the Sabbath), is done in part *l'zecher l'tziat mitzrayim* (as a remembrance of the Exodus from Egypt). Treating the poor and stranger mercifully is related to the fact that the people of Israel were strangers in the land of Egypt and during a time of famine were welcomed and provided for by the Egyptians. Even treating a convert to Judaism kindly is connected to the Exodus because the people of Israel were once strangers in Egypt.

Chukkim

The commandments falling under the category of *chukkim*, under which the dietary laws belong, are more difficult to understand. This is because they are not logical in a straightforward manner. Trying to find "logical" reasons why these observances, especially Kashrut, were commanded has led many to consider a variety of explanations.

One of the greatest rabbis of the medieval period, Rabbi Moses ben Maimon (the *Rambam* or *Maimonides*) stated that "Although all the *chukkim* of the Torah are supra-rational decrees... it is fitting to contemplate them, and whatever can be explained, should be explained."[9] For Rabbi Moses ben Maimon attempting to find the reason why such laws were given was a worthy mental and spiritual endeavor.

Maimonides comments in his philosophical work titled *Moreh Nevuchim* (Guide for the Perplexed) that,

"All of us, the common people as well as the scholars, believe that there is a reason for every precept, although there are commandments the reason of which is unknown to us, and in which the ways of G-d's wisdom are incomprehensible…there are commandments which are called *hukkim*, "ordinances," like the prohibition of wearing garments of wool and linen (*sha'atnez*), boiling meat and milk together, and the sending of the goat [into the wilderness on the Day of Atonement]…but our Sages generally do not think that such precepts have no cause whatever, and serve no purpose; for this would lead us to

---

[9] "The Logic of the Mitzvot." Parshah RSS. Accessed March 03, 2016. http://www.chabad.org/parshah/article_cdo/aid/2797/jewish/The-Logic-of-the-Mitzvot.htm.

assume that G-d's actions are purposeless. On the contrary, they hold that even these ordinances have a cause, and are certainly intended for some use, although it is not known to us; owing either to the deficiency of our knowledge or the weakness of our intellect. Consequently, there is a cause for every commandment: every positive or negative precept serves a useful object; in some cases the usefulness is evident, e.g., the prohibition of murder and theft; in others the usefulness is not so evident, e.g., the prohibition of enjoying the fruit of a tree in the first three years (Lev. xix. 73), or of a vineyard in which other seeds have been growing (Deut. xxii. 9). Those commandments, whose object is generally evident, are called "judgments" (mishpatim); those whose object is not generally clear are called "ordinances" (*hukkim*)."[10]

This attempt has led to various hypotheses. Rabbi Yacov Lipschutz states the following: "Down through the centuries, many have attributed kashruth to either hygienic or social

---

[10] M. Friedlander, trans., Moses Maimonides, *The Guide for the Perplexed* (London: George Routledge & Sons, 1919), 310.

separation purposes."[11] The idea that the dietary laws may reflect beneficial health practices is a widespread view held by many especially those outside the Jewish faith. Others look to the inherent concern to minimize pain to an animal when it is slaughtered. This idea is rooted in various verses found in the Torah that relate a concern for the welfare of animals. For example, an ox that is treading grain should not be muzzled preventing it from consuming some of the food that is right in front of it.[12] Another example is that a mother bird and its eggs should not be eaten on the same day.[13]

Others look for more esoteric rationales for why certain animals are permitted or prohibited. Prohibited fowl, for example, include scavengers and hunters. Eating them, some say, relates the negative qualities of the animals to those who ingest them. In the strictest sense, however, the reasons for the dietary laws are not given. The *Tanya*, the primary book of Hasidic philosophy, states:

"The rationales of the mitzvoth have not been

---

[11] Yacov Lipschutz, *Kashruth*, (Brooklyn: Artscroll Mesorah, 1988), 16.
[12] Deuteronomy 25:4.
[13] Deuteronomy 22:6.

revealed, for they are beyond reason and understanding. Also in those instances in which there has been revealed and explained a certain reason which is apparently comprehensible to us, this is not ... the ultimate reason, for within it is contained an inner, sublime wisdom that is beyond reason and understanding."[14]

The closest explanation or justification is the statement made by G-d preceding the enumeration of the dietary laws, "You will be Holy, for I am Holy." Holiness can be defined as separation or distinction. Observing Kashrut has separated and distinguished the Jewish people for millennia. It is important to note, that in the end, the idea conveyed by the Torah is that every commandment, regardless of its classification, is an act of submission to G-d's will which brings about holiness.

Hasidim and Holiness

---

[14] "The Logic of the Mitzvot." Parshah RSS. Accessed March 03, 2016. http://www.chabad.org/parshah/article_cdo/aid/2797/jewish/The-Logic-of-the-Mitzvot.htm.

If we go back in history and look at an interesting Jewish movement, this may help us understand the thinking behind Kashrut. A Jewish group that first emerged in the 18th century in Eastern Europe and still thrives today provides an interesting rationale for the Jewish dietary laws. This group of ultra-Orthodox Jews (i.e. Jews that believe that the entire Torah in its Written and Oral form were revealed by G-d and that all the commandments are to be strictly observed in accordance with rabbinic interpretation) known as *Hasidim* (i.e. pious ones) promoted the idea of *avodah b'gashmiyut,* which means to serve G-d through physicality (i.e. physical means).[15] That is to say that the service or worship of G-d in a Jewish person's life is accomplished not simply through activities or observances that one might normally characterize or deem as "spiritual" such as prayer or studying Scripture, but rather through physical practices and observances that might otherwise be better

---

[15] "Avodah B'gashmiut - Jewish English Lexicon." Avodah B'gashmiut - Jewish English Lexicon. Accessed March 03, 2016. http://www.jewish-languages.org/jewish-english-lexicon/words/1328.

described as mundane, or everyday actions. In the case of the Hasidim, *avodah b'gashmiyut* was often reflected through physical activities such as dancing, singing, and swaying in prayer. The idea was to make use of the human body and its normal activities vehicles of divine service. The *Hasidim* believed and still do that everything that G-d has created contains a spark of the divine. A wooden table, for example, contains a spark of the divine. How? Because G-d created trees from which wood is derived. A simple wooden table can be elevated to divine service by using it for a holy purpose. Draping a cloth over it and using it for example, for a Shabbat meal (Sabbath meal) is one such way of doing so.

The concept, however, extends far beyond these activities to every aspect of Jewish life and is tied in part to the Jewish idea of creating a *mikdash me'at* – a mini sanctuary in Jewish homes reflective of the sanctity of the *Bet HaMikdash*, the great Temple that once stood in Jerusalem.

Now eating food is a necessity for human survival. While eating food doesn't seem like a spiritual activity, Judaism believes every action is an opportunity to elevate the soul. While *Hasidim* emphasized worship through physical means, they were not the inventors of this concept. This idea is rooted in the Torah itself, the central text of Judaism, where everything from sexual relations, business dealings, agricultural cycles, war, and much more was to be practiced in accordance with the Torah's prescriptions. One area in which a Torah lifestyle was to be felt on an everyday level is Kashrut. The dietary laws are very much connected to the Jewish idea of holiness or separation. According to the Torah, the Jewish people were called to be a holy people, a people set apart. The spiritual component of this calling as emphasized by classical perspectives on Jewish tradition is quite strong. As Rabbi Lipschutz states:

> "Each mitzvah (commandment) serves as a constant reminder of this existence. Therefore, even a commonplace function such as physical nourishment, when properly fulfilled, is sacred in nature and sanctifies the human body... the consumption of forbidden foods defiles the holy

spirit, and its sanctity is injured."[16]

Another author, Steve Katz expresses this idea in broader terms. Judaism is concerned with elevating all of the human experience to the service of G-d.

> "Man's total commitment to the service of G-d, according to Judaism, extends over *all areas of life*. For example, Rabbi Yose stated that all our actions should be performed for the sake of G-d (Avot 2:12)"[17]

Rabbi S. Wagschal provides yet another interpretation as to why the laws of *kashrut* were given to the Jewish people. He states:

> "G-d has taught through the words of the Torah that for B'nei Yisroel [the Children of Israel], certain types of nourishment would be detrimental to the fulfillment of their privileged task...The Torah makes demands and sets standards to equip us for our supreme task of making

---

[16] Yacov Lipschutz, *Kashruth* (Brooklyn: Artscroll Mesorah, 1988), 15.
[17] Steven T. Katz, *Jewish Ideas and Concepts* (New York: Schocken Books, 1980), 222.

mind master of the body, which is the culmination of our spiritual goal."[18]

Now regardless of whether a person adopts the view that the laws of Kashrut are divinely inspired in their entirety or instead views them as a cultural aspect of Jewish distinction as many progressively or liberally minded Jews do today, or a mechanism for instilling discipline and restraint in one's life, their importance as a key marker of Jewish life from antiquity through the postmodern era is without question.[19] In short, the dietary laws are a key element in the distinctiveness of the Jewish people. They are part of what makes the Jewish people holy.

---

[18] S. Wagschal, *The New Practical Guide to Kashruth* (Spring Valley: Felheim Publishers, 1991), 1-2.

[19] As Louis Jacob notes in using Kashrut as an example of Torah development, a sound theological approach will entail: "That the dietary laws were not dictated in all their details by G-d to Moses but evolved gradually, frequently in response to outside stimuli. It will see the whole area of Jewish observances as flowing naturally out of Israel's experiences. "Louis Jacobs, *A Jewish Theology* (Springfield: Berhman House, 1973), 224.

CHAPTER 2
THE BASIC OBSERVANCES OF KASHRUT

A complete review of the laws of Kashrut would require a very extensive work far beyond a simple introduction. Nevertheless, the fundamental concepts and observances of Kashrut can be enumerated in a fairly concise fashion. The basic components for each major area are provided, but the reader should remember that the sections below are only intended to serve as a starting point for the novice approaching this subject. No pun intended, but the following should only serve to whet the reader's appetite for learning more!

The observances that are presented are done so from a traditional approach to the question of Kashrut. Differences as in any other area of Jewish law certainly exist between Conservative and Orthodox movements, but there exists at least in theory [an important point to note], a general agreement on the nature of Kashrut and its key components. For those unfamiliar with the differences between modern Jewish denominations, Reform Judaism, and other liberal movements generally emphasize what they consider ethical-moral behavior over ritual observances. Liberal Jewish movements view the laws of Kashrut as a voluntary observance. Liberal Jewish movements generally look at most commandments as voluntary in nature.

I have focused here on the daily issues of Kashrut and have thus omitted various topics such as the prohibition against eating *chametz* (yeast) during *Pesach* (Passover) and all the associated steps necessary to *kasher* a kitchen during this period. I have also kept brief the discussion regarding the laws associated with food grown in the land of Israel. The koshering process associated with utensils is also kept short. The goal is to provide the reader with the basic elements involved in the laws of Kashrut.

Prohibited and Allowed Animals

The Torah allows certain animals to be eaten. Other animals are prohibited. The requirements for determining which animal is fit for consumption will be mentioned shortly. For those animals falling under the category of prohibited, their "meat", as well as their organs, eggs, and milk, are also forbidden.

Animals that are Forbidden from Being Eaten

The Torah in Leviticus 11:3 and Deuteronomy 14:6, provides the characteristics which determine the permissibility of animals for food. The latter verse states:

> "Among the animals, you may eat any one that has cloven hoofs and that brings up its cud."

The critical factor for permitted mammals then is that they possess *both* cloven hooves and chew their cud. Any land mammal that does not have both of these characteristics is forbidden. Once again, Rabbi Moses ben Maimon stated:

> "There are no other domesticated animals or wild beasts in the world that are permitted to be eaten except the ten

species mentioned in the Torah. They are three types of domesticated animals: an ox, a sheep, and a goat, and seven types of wild beasts: a gazelle, a deer, an antelope, an ibex, a chamois, a bison, and a giraffe. [This includes the species] itself and its subspecies, e.g., the wild ox and the buffalo are subspecies of the ox." [20]

While providing the two determining factors, the Torah *specifically* mentions the camel, the rock badger, the hare, and the pig as unfit because each lacks one of the two above-mentioned qualifications. Pigs have cloven hoofs but do not chew the cud. Because pork is widespread, keeping kosher is often identified by people as abstaining from pork.

Acceptable mammals include cattle, sheep, goats, deer, and bison among others. Interestingly as Maimonides states, giraffes are technically kosher, but no Jewish community has ever eaten them to my knowledge, perhaps because of geography or simply

---

[20]"Ma'achalot Assurot - Chapter 1." - Texts & Writings. Accessed March 03, 2016.
http://www.chabad.org/library/article_cdo/aid/968257/jewish/Maachalot-Assurot-Chapter-1.htm.

because the mechanics of slaughtering such a tall animal were so impractical!

Milk and Cheese

In the United States, milk does not technically have to be under rabbinic supervision to be considered kosher. Because of strong regulatory laws, the concern that milk from non-kosher animals would be mixed with cow milk is insignificant. This consideration is not necessarily the case in other countries. For those Jews who prefer that the milking process is overseen by a Jew, supervised milk called *Cholov Yisrael* is used.[21]

Rennet, an enzyme used to harden cheese, is often obtained from non-kosher animals, thus, kosher hard cheese can be difficult to find.

Fish and Other Sea Creatures

---

[21] Eliezer Wolf, *Keeping Kosher in a non-Kosher World* (New York: Toby Press, 1989), 25.

Regarding sea creatures, the Torah in Leviticus 11:9 and Deuteronomy 14:9-10, stipulates that they must possess fins and scales in order to be acceptable. The latter passage states:

> "These ye may eat of all that are in the waters: whatsoever hath fins and scales may ye eat; and whatsoever hath not fins and scales ye shall not eat; it is unclean unto you."

A fish can be considered kosher by visual inspection. [22] Consequently, sea creatures such as lobsters, crayfish, oysters, clams, shark, squid, octopus, shrimp, and crabs are forbidden. Popular fish such as tuna, carp, salmon, and herring are all acceptable. Catfish and swordfish which lack scales are not acceptable. It is also important to note that the scales must be able to be detached from the skin. [23]

Chopped fish, fish paste, smoked fish, and frozen fish without skin must have a marker identifying them as kosher by a recognized rabbinical organization. The mark or symbol is known

---

[22] Eliezer Wolf, *Keeping Kosher in a non-Kosher World* (New York: Toby Press, 1989), 19.
[23] S. Wagschal, *The New Practical Guide to Kashruth* (Spring Valley: Felheim Publishers, 1991), 11.

as a *hechsher*. It's also important to note that some fish such as carp may have insects or worms in their head, mouth, or gills. They may also cling to the skin. Worms can also be found in the entrails or in the flesh of the fish and hence inspection is often required. [24] As will be noted shortly, most insects are prohibited, so the aforementioned examination is important.

In cases where no kosher fish stores are available, fish may be purchased at a non-kosher store if the fish is recognizable as kosher and has not been salted. In addition, if the store does not allow you to bring a kosher knife to cut the fish with, the area that a non-kosher knife makes contact with should be scraped. [25]

Permitted and Prohibited Fowl

Especially in the case of birds, we are dependent on the Oral Torah to define what the Biblical Hebrew terms actually mean. The Torah does not provide a clear basis or characteristics which distinguish acceptable birds from prohibited ones. Those

---

[24] Ibid., 31.
[25] Eliezer Wolf, *Keeping Kosher in a non-Kosher World* (New York: Toby Press, 1989), 20.

permitted are based on tradition related through the Talmud. In this case, the Torah enumerates those birds that are prohibited. Permitted fowl include chicken, geese, ducks, and turkeys (according to most opinions)[26]. Interestingly, those birds that are prohibited are generally all birds of prey or scavengers and hence many rabbis have concluded that this was the likely basis of differentiation. After the slaughtering procedure has been completed, the process of removing feathers should be done before salting. Hot water cannot be used to remove feathers to avoid any cooking from happening before the meat has been salted.

Insects

On the matter of insects, the Torah in Leviticus 11:20-23 enumerates a handful of bugs that are permitted.

"All winged swarming things that go upon all fours are a detestable thing unto you. Yet these may ye eat of all winged swarming things that go upon all fours, which

---

[26] Yacov Lipschutz, *Kashruth* (Brooklyn: Artscroll Mesorah, 1988), 19.

have jointed legs above their feet, wherewith to leap upon the earth; even these of them ye may eat: the locust after its kinds, and the bald locust after its kinds, and the cricket after its kinds, and the grasshopper after its kinds. But all winged swarming things, which have four feet, are a detestable thing unto you."

The Sages of the Jewish people, however, are no longer certain which bugs are actually referred to so all insects are generally forbidden except in a few communities. Most Jews are probably not that upset at this prohibition!

Insects are generally classified into three categories. The first are insects that live in seas, rivers, and other bodies of water. The second category consists of insects that live in the ground or home as well as those that live in fruits and vegetables. The last category includes flying insects like flies or mosquitos. [27]

---

[27] Reuven Amar, *The Sephardic Kitzur Shulchan Aruch* (Jerusalem: Reuven Amar, 2007), 329.

Kosher Slaughtering

Those mammals and fowl that are deemed permitted to eat must be ritually slaughtered in accordance with Jewish law (Halakhah) through a process known as *shechitah*.[28] The goal is for the maximum amount of blood to be drained as possible. The process is derived from Deuteronomy 12:20-121 which states:

> "When the L-RD thy G-d shall enlarge thy border, as He hath promised thee, and thou shalt say: 'I will eat flesh', because thy soul desireth to eat flesh; thou mayest eat flesh, after all the desire of thy soul. If the place which the L-RD thy G-d shall choose to put His name there be too far from thee, *then thou shalt kill of thy herd and of thy flock, which the L-RD hath given thee, as I have commanded thee,*

---

[28] Deuteronomy 12:21. Rabbi Moses ben Maimon adds "We were commanded concerning all of these factors in the Torah with the verse [Deuteronomy 12:21]: "And you shall slaughter from your cattle... as I commanded you." All of these factors were commanded to us orally as is true with regard to the remainder of the Oral Law which is called "the mitzvah," as we explained in the beginning of this text. "Shechitah - Chapter 1." - Texts & Writings. Accessed March 03, 2016. http://www.chabad.org/library/article_cdo/aid/971827/jewish/Shechitah-Chapter-1.htm.

and thou shalt eat within thy gates, after all the desire of thy soul."

The actual process is not actually described in the Written Torah. Once again, the Oral Torah provides the details for this process. The *shochet* (ritual slaughterer) performs the slaughter by using a quick, deep stroke across the throat using a perfectly sharp blade with no nicks or jaggedness. The *shochet* is not just a regular butcher; he must be a pious man, well-trained in Jewish law, relating to Kashrut. Without elaborating too deeply there are various areas of disqualification during the process of *shechitah*.[29] This method is often regarded as a painless method and causes unconsciousness in the animal within seconds.

A major concern of the process of *shechitah* is that it ensures a speedy, full draining of the blood. The concern for the draining of blood and the prohibition against its consumption is derived from Leviticus 7:26-27 and Leviticus 17:10-14. The former states:

---

[29] Yacov Lipschutz, *Kashruth* (Brooklyn: Artscroll Mesorah, 1988), 20-21.

"And ye shall eat no manner of blood, whether it be of fowl or of beast, in any of your dwellings. Whosoever it be that eateth any blood, that soul shall be cut off from his people."

The Torah provides the rationale for this commandment, by noting that eating blood is forbidden because the life or the soul of the animal is contained in the blood. The prohibition applies to the blood of birds and mammals, though not to the blood of fish. [30] However, fish blood removed from the fish should not be eaten. The concern here is *marat ha'ayin*, the appearance of evil. The prohibition necessitates the removal of all blood from the meat of kosher animals.

Other procedures (depending on the type of meat) such as salting or broiling are also used to eliminate the presence of any remaining blood. Meat is kashered by carefully rinsing all blood. The meat is then salted with medium sized grain salt on all sides. The salted meat is then placed on a grate or slanted board for

---

[30] Reuven Amar, *The Sephardic Kitzur Shulchan Aruch* (Jerusalem: Reuven Amar, 2007), 324.

approximately one hour. This allows the remaining blood to drip down. After this, the salt is removed and the meat is rinsed three times in water. The meat is rubbed by hand to remove any remaining salt or blood.[31]

After the slaughtering process is completed and the majority of the blood drained, the remaining blood is removed through various methods including a process known as *Nikur* which involves the excising of the veins, arteries, and forbidden fats.[32] These additional methods include cooking the meat by broiling or by following a process of soaking and salting. The liver is the only exception to the rule in that it may only be kashered by broiling or roasting. The reason for this lies in the fact that it contains so much blood and has such complex blood vessels. The liver is sliced vertically as well as horizontally and then roasted. After this is accomplished it can be cooked as long as it was washed previously.[33]

---

[31] Reuven Amar, *The Sephardic Kitzur Shulchan Aruch* (Jerusalem: Reuven Amar, 2007), 326.

[32] Yacov Lipschutz, *Kashruth* (Brooklyn: Artscroll Mesorah, 1988), 26.

[33] Reuven Amar, *The Sephardic Kitzur Shulchan Aruch* (Jerusalem: Reuven Amar, 2007), 327.

The soaking process must be completed within 72 hours after slaughter has occurred, and before any freezing or grinding occurs. Meat that has not been kashered within 72 hours of slaughtering is referred to as *Oh'ver*. The soaking time typically lasts between half to one full hour, though unusual circumstances may allow the time to be shortened.[34] If 72 hours have passed, the only method available to koshering meat is by roasting.[35] In the United States, most kosher butchers and kosher frozen food vendors take care of the soaking and salting process. If Kashrut were to be summarized to a handful of commandments, the prohibition against blood would be among them.

Eggs and Blood

The concern for the presence of blood does not end with meat itself, but also extends to an egg that contains a blood spot. Such an egg may not be eaten.[36] If the blood spot can be removed and

---

[34] Ibid., 326.
[35] Ibid., 325.
[36] Yacov Lipschutz, *Kashruth* (Brooklyn: Artscroll Mesorah, 1988), 51.

the yolk remains intact, it is permissible to eat the egg.[37] A recommended procedure for checking is to break an egg into a glass or cup and check it before proceeding. Following this technique is recommended, since if an egg is found to have a blood-stain while in a heated pan, the pan becomes non-kosher as well and cannot be used until it undergoes a process called *kashering* which will be explained later.

Diseased Animals

The Torah also prohibits the consumption of animals that die of natural causes or that were killed by other animals.[38] The rabbis extended the Torah's prohibitions by requiring that animals must have no disease or defects in its organs at the time of slaughter. These restrictions do not apply to fish but only to flocks and herds. The reason for this is found in Numbers 11:22 which only specifies land animals and birds.

---

[37] Reuven Amar, *The Sephardic Kitzur Shulchan Aruch* (Jerusalem: Reuven Amar, 2007), 324.
[38] Deuteronomy 14:21.

"If flocks and herds be *slain* for them, will they suffice them? Or
if all the fish of the sea be gathered together for them, will they
suffice them?"

Kosher slaughterhouses have largely moved to a stricter level of
Kashrut, often referred to as *glatt,* meaning smooth. This level of
Kashrut requires an examination of the lungs of cattle (after
slaughter), to conclude whether the lungs are free from adhesions.
If the lungs are indeed free from any defects, or adhesions, the
animal is regarded as *glatt.* An animal not meeting these
requirements is generally kosher but does not merit the
designation of being *glatt.*[39] *Glatt* kosher has become increasingly
common in recent years and most meat, especially in the United
States, meets these standards.

Forbidden Fats and Nerves

In addition to the concern for blood, a number of other restrictions
are observed. The sciatic nerve and its adjoining blood vessels

---

[39] Yacov Lipschutz, *Kashruth* (Brooklyn: Artscroll Mesorah, 1988), 24-25.

may not be eaten according to the Torah's prohibition in Genesis 32:33:

> "Therefore, the children of Israel eat not the sinew of the thigh-vein which is upon the hollow of the thigh, unto this day; because he touched the hollow of Jacob's thigh, even in the sinew of the thigh-vein."

In the verses preceding the above section, the Torah relates that the patriarch Jacob fought with an unknown angelic figure. This angel struggled with Jacob and finally vanquished him by hitting Jacob's hip socket. This dietary commandment is specifically observed for the purpose of remembering Jacob's struggle. It is one of the few dietary commandments that is connected to a historical event and this commandment is an example of the type of commandments referred to as *Eidot*.

In the United States, the process of removing this nerve is time-consuming and not considered to be cost-effective. This has led kosher slaughterhouses to simply sell the hind quarters to their non-kosher counterparts. *Chelev* or *Chailev*, a certain kind of fat surrounding the vital organs and the liver may not be eaten according to the Torah's prescription in Leviticus 7:22-23 which states:

> "And the L-RD spoke unto Moses, saying: Speak unto the children of Israel, saying: Ye shall eat no fat, of ox, or sheep, or goat."

Kosher butchers remove this.[40] The prohibition against eating fat does not apply to fowl.

Fruits and Vegetables

All fruits and vegetables are acceptable, but they must be thoroughly inspected for prohibited insects. Because many fruits and vegetables are prone to their presence they should be checked thoroughly to ensure that they contain no insects. Worms often burrow themselves into a fruit. This is particularly true for apricots, peaches, plums, cherries, and dates. Because of this, taking a bite out of the whole fruit without inspecting the inside is

[40] Yacov Lipschutz, *Kashruth* (Brooklyn: Artscroll Mesorah, 1988), 30.

prohibited.[41] Other types of fruit are less prone towards this and do not require special examination. Examples of these include oranges, coconuts, tangerines, most pears, apples, bananas, tomatoes, and potatoes.[42] Other fruits like figs, ground nuts, olives, strawberries, and most berries are also of concern and need a general examination.[43]

Many vegetables are susceptible to insects. This is especially true for vegetables like celery, asparagus, scallions, mushrooms, peas in the pod, dried peas, cabbage, lettuce, herbs, broccoli, radishes, and cauliflower. For vegetables like broccoli and cauliflower, a soaking process in water can be used. The rise of organic farming actually increases the concern over insects. Since organic farming generally avoids conventional pesticides, checking for insects becomes even more important.

As a practical concern, this issue presents one of the problems in eating in non-kosher establishments including vegetarian

---

[41] S. Wagschal, *The New Practical Guide to Kashruth* (Spring Valley: Felheim Publishers, 1991), 27.
[42] Ibid., 26.
[43] Ibid., 26.

restaurants. Despite the fact that vegetarian entrees may be theoretically eaten, the lack of certainty regarding the process used to clean fruits and vegetables makes them suspect. There are also other concerns such as how they are prepared and with what utensils, etc. This will be addressed in a subsequent chapter.

CHAPTER 3
SEPARATION OF MEAT AND DAIRY

Perhaps one of the most confusing aspects of the laws of Kashrut relates to the separation between meat and dairy. The Torah stipulates the prohibition on "boiling a kid in its mother's milk" three different times.[44] According to Jewish tradition, the repetition of this prohibition is interpreted as follows: The first mention refers to the ban of cooking the meat of a kosher animal with the milk of a kosher animal. The second repetition refers to the eating this mixture. The last reiteration refers to not deriving benefit from such a combination.[45] The Oral Torah views this prohibition as applying to eating any meat and dairy together,

---

[44] Exodus 23:19; Exodus 34:26; Deuteronomy 14:21.
[45] Eliezer Wolf, *Keeping Kosher in a non-Kosher World* (New York: Toby Press, 1989), 37.

...rdless of whether the meat is goat or not. Subsequent rabbinic legislation extended this proscription to not eating milk and poultry together for the sake of avoiding *marat ha'ayin,* the appearance of evil and also to keep someone from unintentionally forgetting that eating meat and milk was prohibited. All types of cooking, baking, roasting, or frying of meat and dairy are prohibited.[46] The ban against mixing milk and meat also includes any milk-derived product. The same is true for meat derived products. Eating fish and dairy together, however, is allowed. In addition, it is also permissible to eat dairy and eggs together.

The prohibition against mixing milk and meat extends to the utensils as well as the pots and pans in which they are cooked or served. The concern for mixing also applies to dishwashers, sinks, towels, and sponges. This reality causes many families to maintain at least two sets of pots, pans, and dishes.[47] There are Jewish communities from Mediterranean origin however, that use glass instead of separate plates in accordance with the opinion of Rabbi

---

[46] Reuven Amar, *The Sephardic Kitzur Shulchan Aruch* (Jerusalem: Reuven Amar, 2007), 331.
[47] Yacov Lipschutz, *Kashruth* (Brooklyn: Artscroll Mesorah, 1988), 43-44.

Joseph Karo, who is known as the *Maran*. Glass does not absorb particles as do other types of materials. This is also true for Pyrex and Duralex.[48] A meat dish can be served on a glass dish. It can then be washed thoroughly and used to serve another person a dairy item. As a practical matter, this approach greatly simplifies the logistical and financial process for families observing the separation of meat and dairy, although some families still choose to keep glass plates for each type of food.[49] Many Sephardic Jews also refrain from eating fish and meat together. This prohibition is based on the Talmud (Pesachim 76b) which states that eating the two of these together poses a health risk.

The prohibition on eating milk and meat together is rabbinically extended not simply to not eating the two at the same meal. A separation of time between their consumption is also required. When eating dairy after eating meat, what ethnocultural Jewish community one belongs to is the key factor. Jews from various regions often wait for different amounts of time when eating meat

---

[48] Reuven Amar, *The Sephardic Kitzur Shulchan Aruch* (Jerusalem: Reuven Amar, 2007), 335.
[49] Ibid., 335.

after dairy. The Jewish community of Holland, for example, observes a delay of only one hour. The custom of only waiting one hour to eat dairy after eating meat is also extended to nursing mothers or a mother that just gave birth within the last thirty days by some communities.[50] In Germany, the practice is 3 hours. Other communities wait 4 hours. Many Orthodox Jews follow a delay of six hours after meat before eating a dairy product.[51]

In the case of someone who has eaten a dairy item and then intends to eat meat, there is usually a requirement for a person to cleanse their mouth first. This can be accomplished by chewing bread or a fruit. After this, they should rinse their mouth with water.[52]

The Need for Separation

The lapse in time is intended to keep meat and dairy particles from mixing together. This is because fatty residues and meat

---

[50] Reuven Amar, *The Sephardic Kitzur Shulchan Aruch* (Jerusalem: Reuven Amar, 2007), 333.
[51] Ibid., 333.
[52] Ibid., 334.

particles have a tendency to cling to the mouth. When eating dairy first and then continuing with meat, most opinions require that a person needs only to rinse their mouth and/or eat a neutral solid like bread. [53] Fish, eggs, fruits, vegetables, as well as grains can be eaten with either meat or dairy.

Whenever a person is working on a milk or meat dish and then switches to the other type of food, a person should wash his or her hands to avoid contaminating the food or plates. [54] A tablecloth that has been used for one type of meal e.g. meat should be changed if a dairy meal will be served next. Salt and sugar containers used during one meal should not be used at a different type of meal.

---

[53] Yacov Lipschutz, *Kashruth* (Brooklyn: Artscroll Mesorah, 1988), 43.
[54] S. Wagschal, *The New Practical Guide to Kashruth* (Spring Valley: Felheim Publishers, 1991), 37, 39.

CHAPTER 4
UTENSILS AND THE LAWS OF KASHRUT

As was mentioned in the section on eating and mixing milk and meat, the aforementioned prohibitions as well general bans on non-kosher food, impact the various utensils and cookery used in regular preparation.

All utensils including pots, pans, plates, flatware, dishwashers, as well as counter tops must be kosher. This implies that a utensil derives its kosher designation as either meat, dairy, or *pareve* (neutral) from the food that is cooked in it or eaten from it. This designation is of concern, since mixing utensils designated for one type of food with another will transmit this mixture's status (i.e. dairy or meat) back to the next food that is cooked in it or served on it. This transfer of status, however, occurs only in the presence of heat, or extended contact. For Ashkenazic Jews, dishwashers require either separate dish racks or running the dishwasher in between meat and dairy loads. Some Sephardic Jews allow mixed loads as long as soap is placed inside the dishwasher as well as the normal compartment for soap. This practice is based on the view of Rabbi Joseph Karo.[55]

Stove tops and sinks often become non-kosher, because they come in contact with both meat and dairy in the presence of heat. Dish pans are recommended to avoid soaking plates and utensils directly in the sink. Furthermore, separate spoon rests and holders are also suggested when putting things down on a stove top. Ideally, separate towels and pot holders should be used for meat and dairy.

To *kasher* utensils, two methods are available. The first method is to place the utensil in question in a pot of boiling water. The second which is more complicated and less common is to heat the

---

[55] "DailyHalacha.com." Daily HALACHA by Rabbi Eli Mansour. Accessed March 03, 2016.
https://www.dailyhalacha.com/displayRead.asp?readID=810.

utensil to the point that it becomes red. It's important to note that only utensils made from wood or metal can be koshered.

An oven that has been used for non-kosher food should be cleaned thoroughly. It should then be set at the highest temperature possible, or the self- cleaning cycle for at least one hour. The racks in the oven can be kashered by running the self-cleaning cycle. Some families opt to kasher their ovens by use of an industrial blowtorch.[56] This approach obviously requires great care and only someone with experience should undertake this.

Any utensil that has been previously owned by a non-Jew and is now owned by a Jew should be *toveled* (immersed) in a *mikveh* (ritual immersion pool) before being used.[57] If a mikveh is not available, ritual immersion can also take place in a natural water source such as a well, a river, a lake, or the sea. The process essentially sanctifies the utensils. There are a variety of rules regarding when immersion can occur and what should be done

---

[56] Eliezer Wolf, *Keeping Kosher in a non-Kosher World* (New York: Toby Press, 1989), 23-24.
[57] Reuven Amar, *The Sephardic Kitzur Shulchan Aruch* (Jerusalem: Reuven Amar, 2007), 341.

when multiple items are being immersed. A *berachah*, a ritual blessing is pronounced before the immersion takes place. The text of the blessing is "Blessed are You, L-rd our G-d, King of the Universe, Who has sanctified us with His commandments, and commanded us regarding the immersion of a vessel."

CHAPTER 5
BREAD AND WINE

Bread and wine formed a unique staple in most Near Eastern diets and their continuing importance remains visible in Jewish religious life through their constant presence and the various *berachot* (Hebrew blessings) associated with them. The concern for the ingredients used in bread which often include dairy products and a large variety of modern ingredients continues the need for bread being made under appropriate supervision. This concern also includes the observance of the commandment to observe the procedure of *challah*.

Separation of Challah

Most Jews think of *challah* as delicious, braided bread eaten at Friday night Sabbath dinners and holidays. The term *challah*, however also refers to the commandment of separating a portion of the dough. This portion of dough is set aside as a tithe for the *Cohanim* (priests). In Hebrew, this commandment is referred to as *hafrashat challah*. The source for this commandment is found in Numbers 15:17-21 which states:

"And the L-RD spoke unto Moses, saying: speak unto the children of Israel, and say unto them: When ye come into the land whither I bring you, then it shall be, that, when ye eat of the bread of the land, ye shall set apart a portion for a gift unto the L-RD. Of the first of your dough ye shall *set apart* a cake for a gift; as that which is set apart of the threshing-floor, so shall ye set it apart. Of the first of your dough, ye shall give unto the L-RD a portion for a gift throughout your generations."

The predominant practice among those observing this commandment is to burn the portion that would normally have been given to a *Cohen* (priest), although giving the *challah* to a

Cohen for consumption is technically permitted outside of Israel. Other individuals place the portion in two plastics bags and then discarding.[58] *Challah* is one of the various portions that was biblically allotted to the priesthood as a means of sustenance. This was because the *Cohanim* (priests) were expected to be involved with the daily service and upkeep of the Temple and providing instruction in the Torah. When the Children of Israel entered into the Land of Canaan, the priests were not assigned land as were the other tribes of Israel.

The requirement to separate challah applies only to dough prepared from a flour derived from wheat, barley, oat, spelt, or rye. The minimal quantity of dough whose preparation requires the separation of *challah* along with the recitation of the corresponding *beracha* (Hebrew blessing) is around 1.64 kg. A batch of dough weighing between 2 lb 11oz (1.23 kg) and 3 lb 11oz (1.666 kg) does not require a *beracha* (Hebrew blessing) to be recited but the *challah* portion is separated.

---

[58] Eliezer Wolf, *Keeping Kosher in a non-Kosher World* (New York: Toby Press, 1989), 27.

Today, the eating of *challah* by a *Cohen* in the Land of Israel is actually forbidden by the Torah. This is due to the absence of the components necessary for ritual purity to be completely effected. While the commandment in its fullest sense cannot be observed, *separating* challah ensures in order that the commandment will not be forgotten. This tendency of observing a commandment partially is done for various commandments given the absence of a functioning Temple in Jerusalem and the associated sacrificial system that once existed.

Most Jews living outside the Land of Israel burn the *challah* portion. Technically, it is permitted outside of the land of Israel to give the *challah* to a *Cohen* to eat. The *Cohen* to whom the challah is given should have immersed in a *mikvah* (ritual immersion pool). This practice is not widespread but is another attempt to maintain the commandment alive as much as possible.

Supervision of Wine

In the case of wine, the concern for appropriate supervision is heightened due to its ancient connection to religious rites. The prohibition is connected to the Torah's concern over wine libations Deuteronomy 32:36-38:

"For the L-RD will judge His people, and repent Himself for His servants; when He seeth that their stay is gone, and there is none remaining, shut up or left at large. And it is said: Where are their gods, the rock in whom they trusted; Who did eat the fat of their sacrifices, and drank the wine of their drink-offering? let him rise up and help you, let him be your protection."

The major prohibition, however, was expounded in the Talmudic and in the Gaonic period:

"The establishment of the prohibition is explained in the Talmud as a means to eliminate the possibility of use of pagan libations and to prevent Jewish intermarriage and assimilation with followers of other faiths...the scholars of the Gaonic period limited the prohibition of use or benefit to wines of polytheistic non-Jews who worship pagan deities..."[59]

Wine handled by non-Jews even when no suspicion of idolatry existed was also prohibited. Such wine is referred to as *stam yeinam*.[60] The concern over its ritual use in pagan practices continues to this day, though the practice is with few exceptions largely obsolete in regions where idolatry is no longer practiced, though which religions qualify as idolatrous is a subject of great discussion and debate in Jewish circles.

A new emphasis is placed on the concern that wine induces carefreeness and a weakened judgment. Drunkenness can lead to immoral behavior and to intermarriage.[61]

---

[59] Yacov Lipschutz, *Kashruth* (Brooklyn: Artscroll Mesorah, 1988), 74. The Gaonic period refers to the era that followed the closing of the Talmud in the 6th century CE and was made up of the rabbis who headed the great Yeshivot such as Sura and Pumbedita in Babylon. Jewish communities often wrote to the Gaonim (i.e. the Great Ones) of their generation for guidance in Jewish religious matters.

[60] Reuven Amar, *The Sephardic Kitzur Shulchan Aruch* (Jerusalem: Reuven Amar, 2007), 339.

[61] S. Wagschal, *The New Practical Guide to Kashruth* (Spring Valley: Felheim Publishers, 1991), 21.

The prohibition against wine handled by non-Jews extends to all liquids produced from fresh or dried grapes. It includes alcoholic or non-alcoholic beverages and also includes vinegar. Alcoholic beverages derived from wine such as cognac and brandy must be guaranteed as kosher.[62] One method of circumventing the concerns of wine handled by non-Jews is the process of *mevushal*. Mevushal refers to boiling kosher wine or grape juice. Once the process is completed, non-Jewish handling is no longer a concern.[63]

---

[62] Ibid., 23.
[63] Ibid., 24.

CHAPTER 6
FOOD COOKED BY NON-JEWS

In addition to the various categories of acceptable and prohibited food, there is also another area of concern. The involvement of a non-Jew in the food preparation process is problematic. According to Jewish law, a non-Jew may participate in preparing food in a Jewish home, but the actual cooking must be done by a Jew. If a non-Jew does cook food, it must be treated as prohibited.[64] The reason for this lies in the possibility that prohibited food or mixing has occurred. An individual that is not obligated to observe the commandments is considered not to be as scrupulous in their observance even if proper instruction is given. A secondary

---

[64] Reuven Amar, *The Sephardic Kitzur Shulchan Aruch* (Jerusalem: Reuven Amar, 2007), 337.

consideration is the need to prevent intimate relationships from developing. Once again, the concern is that the possibility of intermarriage may occur.[65] The importance of food in forging and maintaining family relationships is highlighted by this fact.

Cooking by a non-Jew as understood by Jewish law is divided into three steps. The first is the process of "lighting the fire" or its contemporary equivalent. The second is the process by which the food is placed in contact with the fire. The last is the step at which food becomes eatable due to the fire. According to Jewish law, *bishul nochri,* cooking by a non-Jew, only happens when a non-Jew performs the entire cooking process. If a Jew carries out, at least, one of the processes, the food is acceptable assuming that all the other aspects of kashrut are observed.[66] Many Sephardic Jews require that in addition to lighting the flame or turning on the

---

[65] S. Wagschal, *The New Practical Guide to Kashruth* (Spring Valley: Felheim Publishers, 1991), 33.
[66] Ibid., 36.

burner, a Jew must actually place the food on the burner. A non-Jew can then continue with the cooking process.[67]

Eating in Non-Kosher Restaurants

Depending on where a person lives, few if any kosher establishments may be available. Many people believe that eating in a vegetarian restaurant is the second best thing when a non-kosher establishment is unavailable. In certain respects, this is true. For example, it is permissible to eat a fruit salad or a vegetable salad in a vegetarian restaurant provided that certain requirements are met. For example, the utensils, as well as the plates used to prepare the fruit or vegetables, must be clean from non-kosher food. In addition, the vegetables must be free of insects. Salads cannot have grape juice or vinegar since these products must have been processed under rabbinic supervision. Lastly, the salad cannot contain onions or radishes.[68] Cutting an

---

[67] Reuven Amar, *The Sephardic Kitzur Shulchan Aruch* (Jerusalem: Reuven Amar, 2007), 337.

[68] Eliezer Wolf, *Keeping Kosher in a non-Kosher World* (New York: Toby Press, 1989), 19.

onion or radish with a knife that was once used to cut hot non-kosher food renders the onion or radish non-kosher as well.[69]

There are other issues to keep in mind with a vegetarian restaurant, however. Not all food in this type of restaurant is necessarily vegetarian. One example is that of margarine. Some margarine contains animal fat. If this is the case, any pots that have been exposed to the margarine are now rendered non-kosher. Some vegan restaurants use food products made overseas. This often true for soy-related products. The lack of a kosher inspection process raises doubts as to the true content.

Cheese is another consideration since it may contain rennet.[70] For Orthodox Jews, cheese made by non-Jews is forbidden even if it is made without rennet. Many Jews who follow Jewish law as interpreted by the Conservative movement view rennet as so

---

[69] Ibid., 18-19.

[70] Eliezer Wolf, *Keeping Kosher in a non-Kosher World* (New York: Toby Press, 1989), 18.

altered chemically that is no longer maintains the characteristics of "food." In any case, food cooked by a non-Jew is prohibited.[71]

There are other concerns as well. A general comment regarding the challenges faced with processed foods should be made. Foods containing gelatin, rennet, bone phosphate, pepsin, fats, and oils which are not wholly composed of vegetable origins, glycerin, glycerol, and other items contain non-kosher ingredients.[72] As you can see, while a vegetarian restaurant may be the safest option where kosher establishments are unavailable, there are plenty of things to worry about for the individual striving to keep kosher.

---

[71] Ibid., 18.
[72] S. Wagschal, *The New Practical Guide to Kashruth* (Spring Valley: Felheim Publishers, 1991), 5.

CHAPTER 7
PRODUCE GROWN IN THE LAND OF ISRAEL

A number of commandments related to *kashrut* are specifically connected to food grown in the land of Israel. For years, these laws were largely inapplicable due to the fact that most Jews lived in the Diaspora. These commandments applied to only a small number of people. With the creation of the modern state of Israel, the application of these commandments is again a concern.

Shemittah

The most significant of these is the commandment of *Shemittah*. *Shemittah* is the Sabbath year. It is also referred to as the sabbatical year. It is the seventh year of the seven-year agricultural cycle required by the Torah for the Land of Israel. During this year, the land is left to lie unplanted. Agricultural activity including plowing, planting, pruning and harvesting, is forbidden by Jewish law. The application of this in the modern State of Israel is a complicated matter. I will not elaborate on this due to the details involved.

A number of other commandments are also related to the Land of Israel. Food grown in the land of Israel may be eaten only after certain separations have taken place. This applies even in cases where the food is eaten outside of the land of Israel. The separations are supposed to be made for a variety of foods including ones that are raw, cooked, dried, or baked. A total of four separations is supposed to be made. The first is referred to as *terumah*. This portion is a quantity allotted to the *Cohanim* (priests). A second separation is *ma'aser rishon*. This is the first tithe and includes ten percent of a crop. This was originally slated for the *Leviim* (the Levites) who assisted the *Cohanim* in their priestly duties.

The third separation was called the *terumat ma'aser*. This separation was a tenth of the *ma'aser* and was supposed to be given to the Levite or *Cohen* (Priest). The last separation was called the *ma'aser sheni* or the *ma'aser oni*. This second *ma'aser* or the tithe of the poor consisted of a tenth of the crop after the *ma'aser rishon* had been taken. This portion was taken during the first, second, fourth, and fifth years of the seven-year agricultural cycle culminating with the observance of *Shemittah*. The portion was eaten by the owner when he visited the Temple in Jerusalem. Portions taken from food grown during the third and sixth year were given to the poor, hence the secondary designation as the tithe of the poor.[73]

Without elaborating too deeply, the portions are separated after the reciting a declaration. In the case of *terumah* and *terumat ma'aser,* the portions are not given to the Levites or to the *Cohanim* (Priests) but are disposed of. This is because of the ritually impure state of modern day Levites and *Cohanim* in the absence of the purifications methods available in the days of the Temple.

Orlah

---

[73] S. Wagschal, *The New Practical Guide to Kashruth* (Spring Valley: Felheim Publishers, 1991), 100.

The Torah also prohibits eating or obtaining benefit from a tree that is in within three years of its being planted. The prohibition extends not only to the fruit, but to all the elements of the tree including the seeds, peels, and branches. A tree within the three year period is referred to as *Orlah*.[74] The prohibition applies to trees grown in the Diaspora and the land of Israel. The application of this law is less stringent in the Diaspora where a doubt regarding the Orlah status of a tree does not render the tree or its fruit prohibited.[75]

The three-year designation is not necessarily three complete years. If a tree, for example, was planted forty-four days before *Rosh Hashanah,* this period counts as the first year. Two additional years must be counted with the third year ending on *Tu B'Shvat*, the beginning of the year for trees.[76]

Once the three year period has ended, the tree and its fruit are still forbidden. The fruit produced from the tree is referred to as *neta*

---

[74] Reuven Amar, *The Sephardic Kitzur Shulchan Aruch* (Jerusalem: Reuven Amar, 2007), 390.
[75] Ibid. 391.
[76] Ibid. 391.

r'vai. According to the Torah, in order to eat this fruit, the owner had to travel to Jerusalem. Ritual purity was also required to the fruit. Since the process for achieving ritual purity is not currently in place, the fruit must be redeemed with a coin or fruit. The blessing associated with the process of redemption is not recited in the Diaspora. The coin or fruit used to redeem the *neta r'vai* must be discarded since the Temple is not in existence at this time.[77]

---

[77] Ibid. 392.

CONCLUSIONS

The laws of Kashrut extend considerably beyond the areas already enumerated. Nevertheless, the general concepts can be found under the subject headings already covered. Like any culture or peoplehood, the laws of Kashrut can be understood in a variety of ways. Yet whatever differences are attributable to the different ethnocultural aspects of Jewish communities around the world, the laws of Kashrut delve far deeper than simple culture can be given credit for. I strongly believe that they reflect the notion of *kedushah*, of holiness or separation frequently expounded upon by the Tanakh (Hebrew Scripture). While the fundamentals of Kashrut are easy to learn, the intricacies become quickly apparent to those who explore the subject deeper. My heartfelt goal is that the reader will have at least gained a basic understanding of one of the fundamental identifiers of Jews who strive to be religiously observant. Questions will inevitably arise and I encourage the eager student to consult the various books listed in the section on resources for further study.

GLOSSARY OF FREQUENTLY USED TERMS

Hebrew (Heb)**; Yiddish** (Yid)**; English** (Eng)

Ashkenazim (Heb)- This term is derived from the Hebrew word *Ashkenaz* which was used in the medieval period to refer to Germany. Today it refers to Jews from Central and Eastern European Jewish backgrounds.

Avodah b'Gashmiyut (Heb) – literally, service through physicality. The term refers to religious worship through ordinary and seemingly mundane things.

Basar (Heb)- meat.

Berachot (Heb)- Blessings said before performing or observing a religious action.

Bet HaMikdash (Heb)- "The Sanctified House." The rabbinic term used to refer to the first and second Temples constructed in Jerusalem.

Bishul Nochri (Heb)- Food cooked by a non-Jew.

B'nai Israel (Heb)- The children of Israel; the Jewish people.

Challah (Heb)-typically refers to special bread eaten on Shabbat and Jewish holidays but is derived from the biblical commandment to remove a portion of the dough and given to the Cohanim (priests).

Chametz (Heb)- leaven/yeast prohibited during Passover.

Chelev/ Chailev (Heb)- a certain kind of fat surrounding the vital organs that is prohibited.

Chukkim (Heb)- The plural of *hok* which is often translated as decrees. These are commandments whose purpose or meaning cannot be logically determined.

Eidot (Heb)- The plural of *eidah* meaning testimonial. It generally refers to a commandment that serves as a reminder of a special event i.e. the Exodus from Egypt.

Geonim (Heb) - The heads of the two great Babylonian, Talmudic Academies of Sura and Pumbedita.

Glatt (Yid)- means smooth and is used in reference to the lack of blemishes or lesions on the lungs of an animal. The term now implies a higher degree of supervision.

Haggadah (Heb)- The telling of the story of Passover.

Halav (Heb)- Milk or milk derived products.

Halakhah (Heb)- the collective body of Jewish law.

Hechsher (Heb)- guaranteed sign of kashrut by a recognized rabbinical authority.

Hasidim (Heb)- Literally "pious ones." An orthodox Jewish movement that began in the 18th century. Its focus is on Jewish mysticism as a critical component of Jewish faith and in its early stages was particularly characterized by joyous worship and belief in the immanent nature of G-d.

Kashering (Eng)- The process of returning a utensil to its previous kosher state.

Kashrut (Heb) - Jewish religious dietary laws derived from the Written and Oral Laws. The term kashrut is derived from the Hebrew word *kasher* meaning fit or acceptable. From the word *kasher*, we derive the word kosher in its English form.

Kiddush (Heb)- i.e. sanctification. Kiddush is recited over a cup of wine or grape juice. It is said on Friday evening and on various other occasions.

Mikdash Me'at (Heb)- A little or miniature sanctuary.

Mishpatim (Heb)-The plural of *mishpat*.The term is generally translated as laws and refers to commandments whose practical benefit for an orderly society are clear.

Pareve (Heb)- Neutral. A food item that can be eaten with milk or meat or with the associated utensils.

Ma'aser/Ma'aser Sheni (Heb)- First and second tithes. They constitute portions of food grown in the land of Israel.

Nikur (Heb)-Porging refers to the removal of certain fats, sinews, sciatic nerve, and veins from a slaughtered meat.

Matzah (Heb) – Unleavened bread eaten during Passover.

Mitzvah (Heb)- commandment.

Mitzvot (Heb) - The commandments of the Written and Oral Law.

Marat Ha'ayin (Heb)- The appearance of evil.

Neta R'vai (Heb)- The fruit of a tree in the fourth year from its initial planting. This fruit must be redeemed in order to be consumed.

Oh'ver (Heb) - Meat that has not been kashered within 72 hours of slaughtering.

Oral Law - Rabbinic Judaism maintains that the Torah was revealed in Written and Oral form. The written text is comprised of the "Books of Moses," The Oral Torah provides the interpretation and implementation of the commandments outlined in the Written Torah.

Orlah (Heb)- A tree within three years of its initial planting. All of the elements of the tree i.e. fruit, seed, branches, etc. are forbidden during this time.

Passover (Eng)/ **Pesach** (Heb)- The biblical holiday commemorating the deliverance of the Jewish people from bondage in the land of Egypt.

Shabbat (Heb)- the Sabbath; the Seventh day of rest.

Seder (Heb)- literally order. Typically refers to the order of Passover meal.

Sephardim (Heb)- This term is derived from the Hebrew word *Sepharad* which was used in the medieval period to refer to the Iberian Peninsula. Today it refers to Jews from Spain, Portugal, North Africa, and the Levant.

Shechitah (Heb)- The process of slaughtering an animal in accordance with Jewish law.

Shemitah (Heb)- The seventh or sabbatical year during which produce grown in the land of Israel is prohibited.

Shochet (Heb)- The ritual slaughter who slaughters meat in accordance with Jewish law.

Shulchan Aruch (Heb) - literally the "Set table"; It is the principal code of Jewish law written in the 16th century and compiled by Rabbi Joseph Karo.

Stam Yeinam (Heb)- refers to any wine handled by non-Jews even in cases where it has not been offered to idols.

Tanakh (Heb)- The Jewish Bible or Hebrew Scriptures. An acronym for Torah/Nevi'im/Kethuvim. The Torah refers to the five books of Moses. The Nevi'im refers to books that are deemed prophetic in nature. Kethuvim refers to the "Writings" which constitute the remaining books not included in the previous two categories.

Tanya (Heb)- Fundamental Hasidic work of Jewish mysticism written by Shneur Zalman of Liadi.

Talmud (Heb) - A central text of Rabbinic Judaism composed of the Mishnah and its commentary, the Gemara.

Tefillin (Heb) - Small black leather boxes containing scrolls of parchment. The scrolls inscribed with verses from the Torah. They are worn by religious Jews during weekday morning prayers.

Terumah (Heb) - A food item given to a priest, as a gift.

Torah (Heb)- means instruction or teaching and specifically refers to the Five Books of Moses (i.e. Genesis, Exodus, Leviticus, Numbers, and Deuteronomy). It is the foundation of Jewish life and Jewish law.

Tovel (Heb)- refers to immersing utensils in a mikveh (pool of water used for ritual purposes).

Treifah (Heb)- derived from the Hebrew word meaning tear or torn. Generally, it refers to food or utensils that are not permitted.

RECOMMENDED RESOURCES
FOR ADDITIONAL STUDY

This book was intended to provide the reader with a brief review of what Kashrut is. To obtain a deeper understanding of Kashrut, a number of excellent resources are available. The books below are a few of the many books that have been published.

Feldheim Publications

Rabbi Moshe Eliyohu Klugman, *The Jewish Kitchen, Expanded 1 Vol. Edition. A comprehensive review of the Halachos pertaining to a Kosher kitchen and Tevilas Keilim.*

Rabbi Zalman Goldstein, *Going Kosher in 30 Days! An Easy Step-By-Step Guide for the Rest of Us.*

Rabbi A. Wiesenfeld, *Kashrus in the Kitchen Q & A: A Comprehensive Question-and-Answer Guide to the Halachos of Meat and Milk.*

Artscroll Mesorah

Shimon Apisdorf, *Kosher for the Clueless but Curious: A fun, fact-filled and spiritual guide to all things kosher.*

Rabbi Binyomin Forst, *The Kosher Kitchen - Feuereisen Edition: A Practical Guide.*

Rabbi Yacov Lipschutz, *Kashruth.*

Toby Press

Pinchas Cohen, *A Practical Guide to the Laws of Kashrut.*

Independent Publishers

Rabbi Eliezer Wolf, *Keeping Kosher in a Non-Kosher World.*

Rabbi Reuven Amar, *The Sephardic Kitzur Shulchan Aruch.*

ABOUT THE AUTHOR

Rabbi Juan Marcos Bejarano Gutierrez is a graduate of the University of Texas at Dallas where he earned a bachelor of science in electrical engineering. He studied at the Siegal College of Judaic Studies in Cleveland and received a Master of Arts Degree with Distinction in Judaic Studies. He completed his doctoral studies at the Spertus Institute for Jewish Learning and Leadership in Chicago in 2015. He studied at the American Seminary for Contemporary Judaism and received rabbinic ordination in 2011 from Yeshiva Mesilat Yesharim. Rabbi Bejarano Gutierrez served as the assistant editor for *HaLapid,* the quarterly publication of the Society for Crypto-Judaic Studies, from 2011-2012. He also served as a board member and treasurer of the Society for Crypto-Judaic Studies from 2011-2013. He has published various articles in *HaLapid, The Journal for Spanish, Portuguese and Italian Crypto-Jews,* and *Apuntes-Theological Reflections from a Hispanic-Latino Context.* He is active in helping individuals who are the descendants of Crypto-Jews and is currently the director of the B'nai Anusim Center for Education.

What is Kosher?

Made in the USA
San Bernardino, CA
10 February 2020